EASY GUITAR WITH NOTES & TAB

ISBN 978-1-4950-5884-4

HAL•LEONARD®

Visit Hal Leonard Online at
www.halleonard.com

Contact us:
Hal Leonard
7777 West Bluemound Road
Milwaukee, WI 53213
Email: info@halleonard.com

In Europe, contact:
Hal Leonard Europe Limited
42 Wigmore Street
Marylebone, London, W1U 2RN
Email: info@halleonardeurope.com

In Australia, contact:
Hal Leonard Australia Pty. Ltd.
4 Lentara Court
Cheltenham, Victoria, 3192 Australia
Email: info@halleonard.com.au

STRUM AND PICK PATTERNS

This chart contains the suggested strum and pick patterns that are referred to by number at the beginning of each song in this book. The symbols ⊓ and ⋁ in the strum patterns refer to down and up strokes, respectively. The letters in the pick patterns indicate which right-hand fingers play which strings.

p = thumb
i = index finger
m = middle finger
a = ring finger

For example; Pick Pattern 2
is played: thumb - index - middle - ring

Strum Patterns   ## Pick Patterns

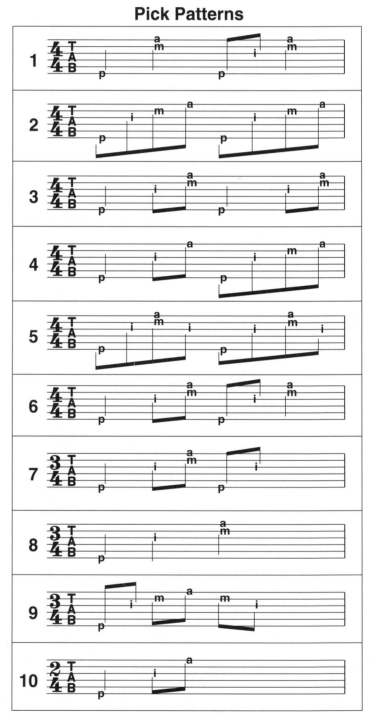

You can use the 3/4 Strum and Pick Patterns in songs written in compound meter (6/8, 9/8, 12/8, etc.).
For example, you can accompany a song in 6/8 by playing the 3/4 pattern twice in each measure.
The 4/4 Strum and Pick Patterns can be used for songs written in cut time (¢) by doubling the note time values in the patterns. Each pattern would therefore last two measures in cut time.

Across the Stars

Love Theme from STAR WARS: EPISODE II - ATTACK OF THE CLONES

Music by John Williams

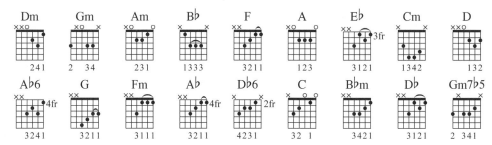

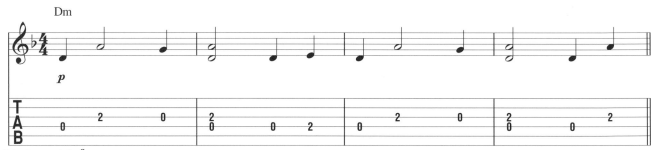

*Strum Pattern: 4
*Pick Pattern: 4

Intro
Moderately slow

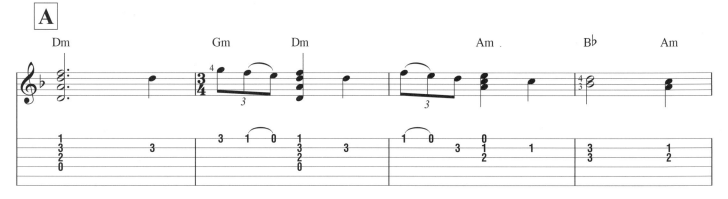

*Use Pattern 8 for ¾ meas.

A

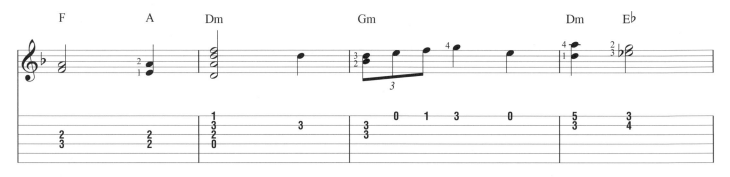

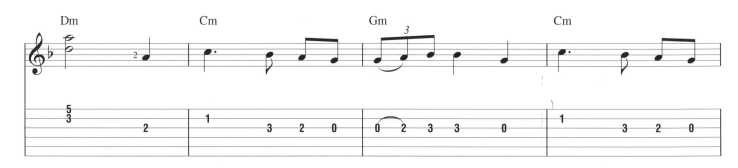

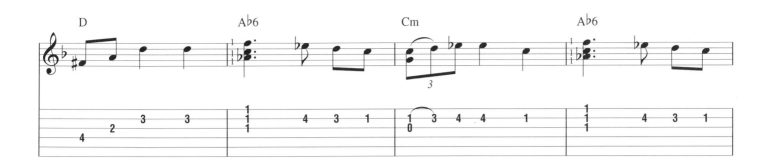

B

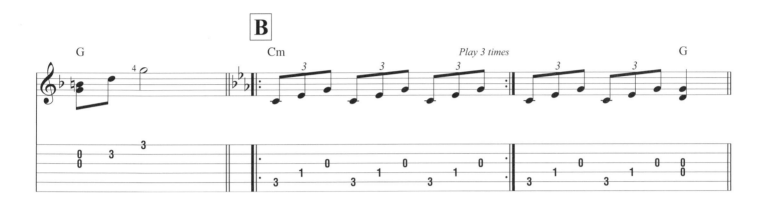

C

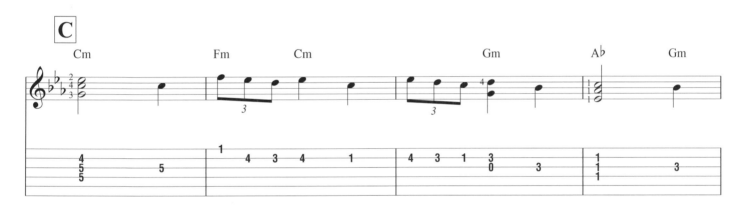

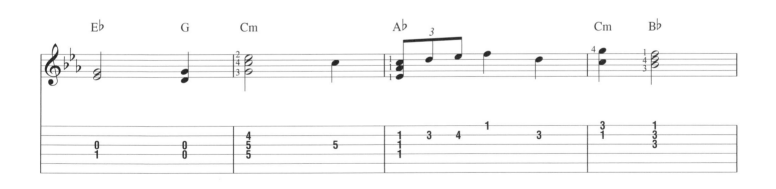

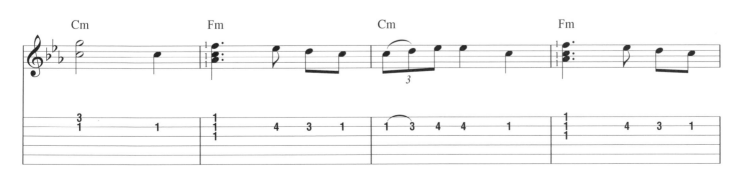

D

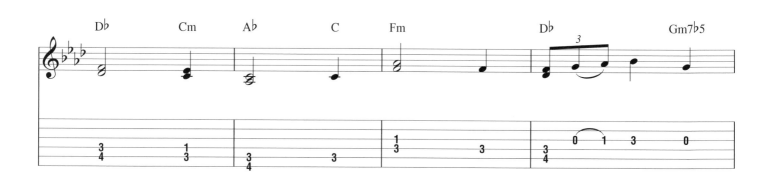

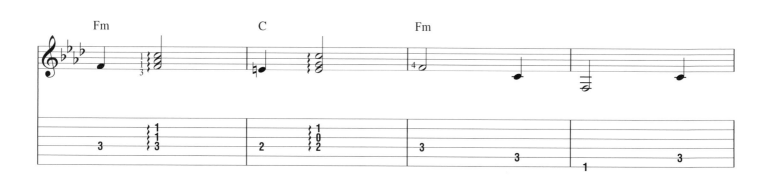

Cantina Band

from STAR WARS: EPISODE IV - A NEW HOPE

Music by John Williams

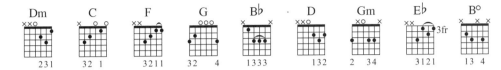

Strum Pattern: 3
Pick Pattern: 3

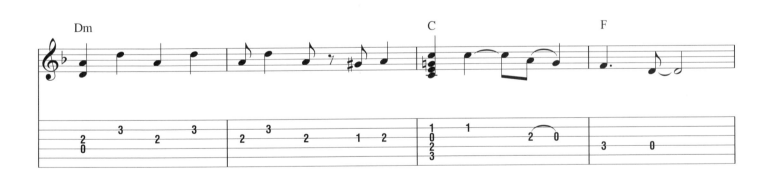

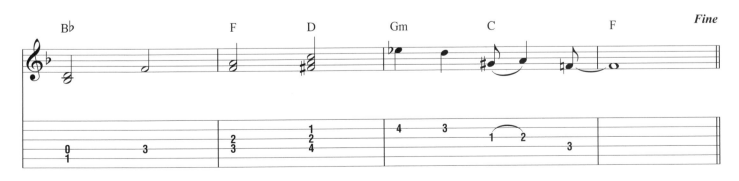

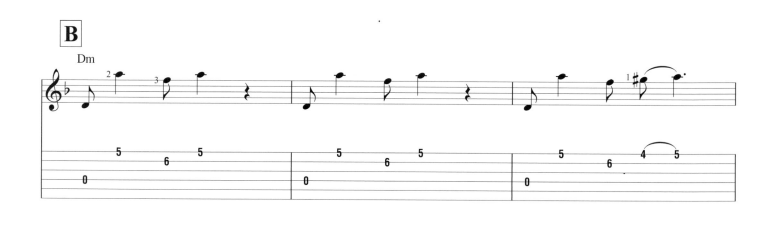

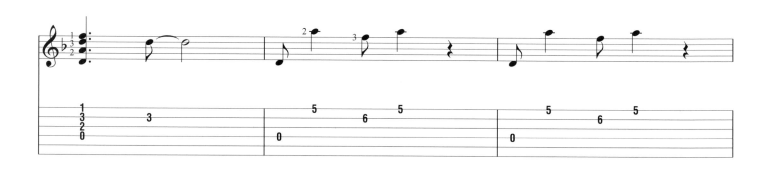

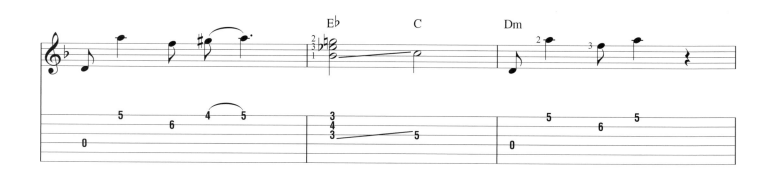

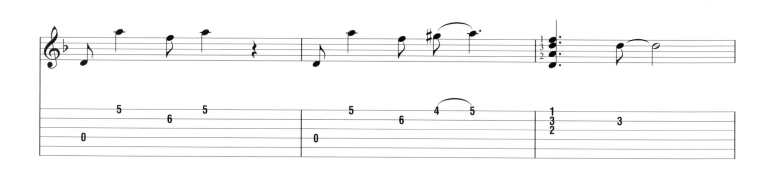

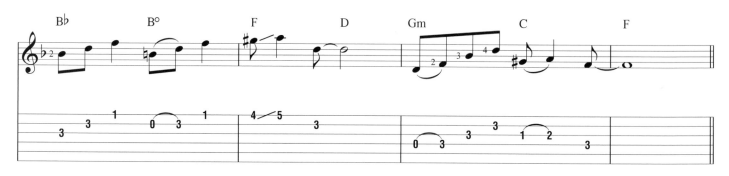

C

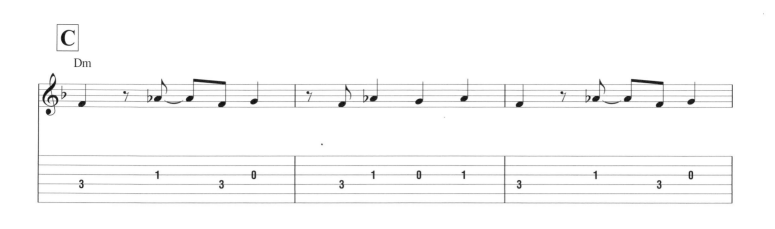

2nd time, D.C. al Fine

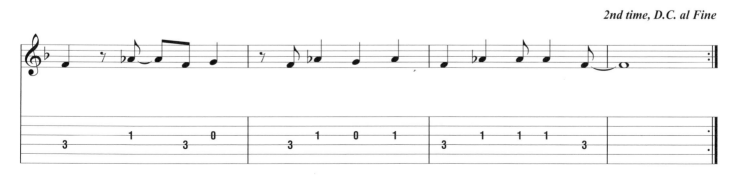

Duel of the Fates

from STAR WARS: EPISODE I - THE PHANTOM MENACE

Music by John Williams

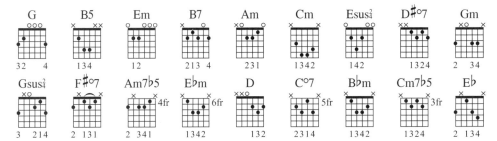

G B5 Em B7 Am Cm Esus²₄ D#°7 Gm

Gsus²₄ F#°7 Am7♭5 E♭m D C°7 B♭m Cm7♭5 E♭

Strum Pattern: 5
Pick Pattern: 1

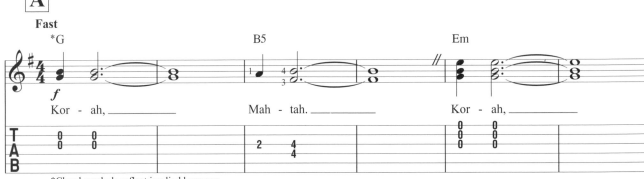

*Chord symbols reflect implied harmony.

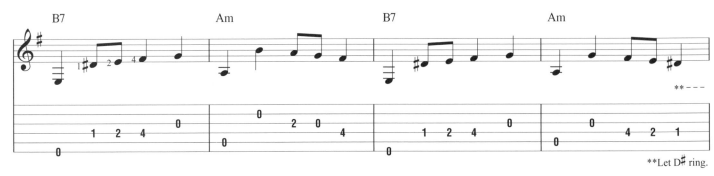

**Let D# ring.

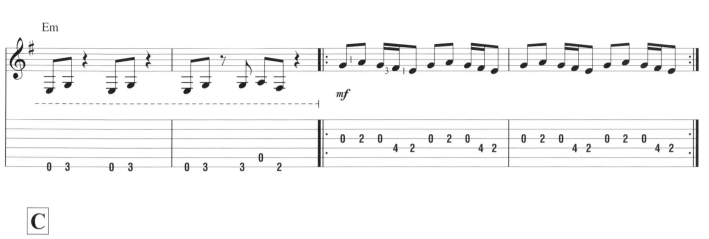

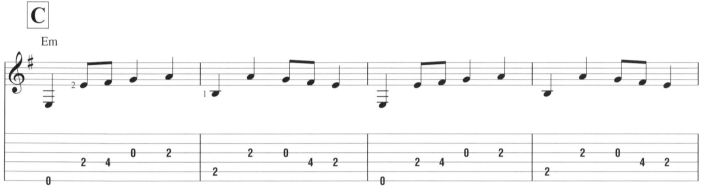

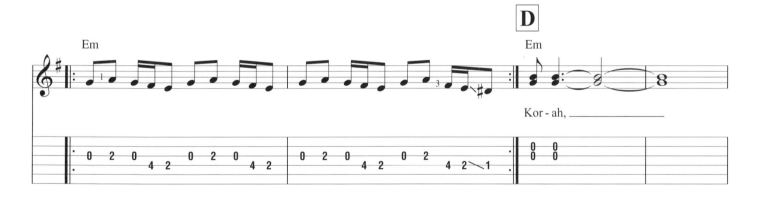

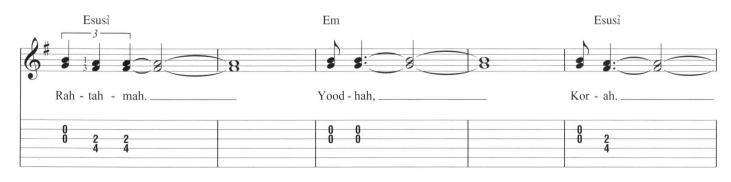

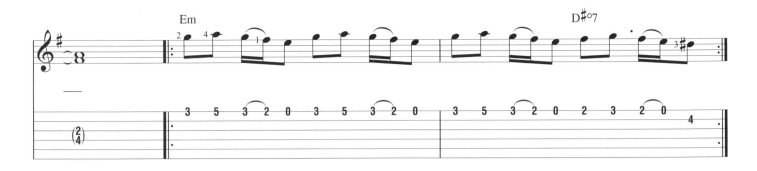

E

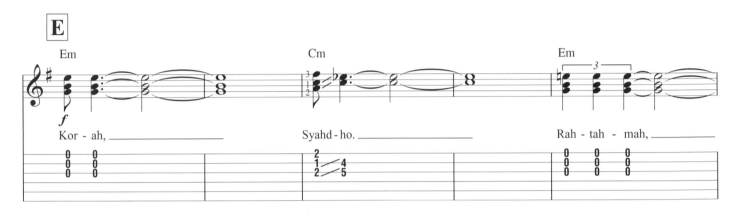

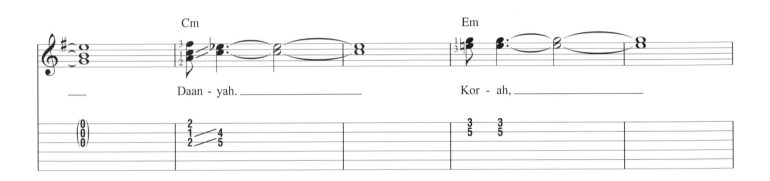

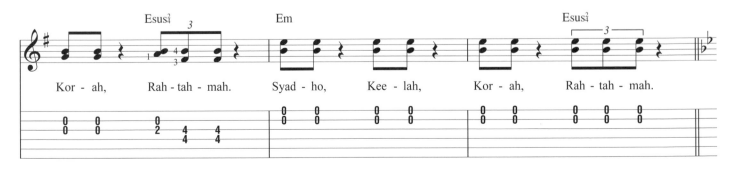

F

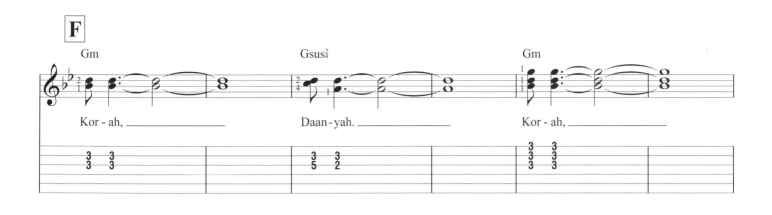

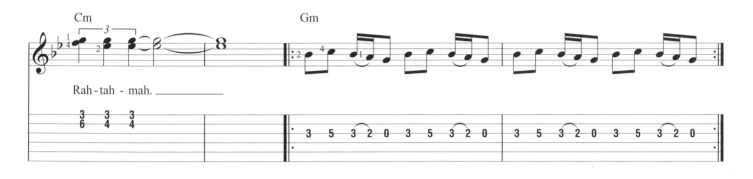

G

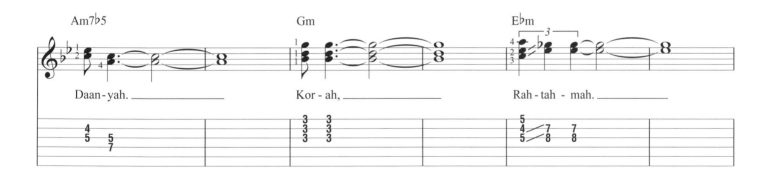

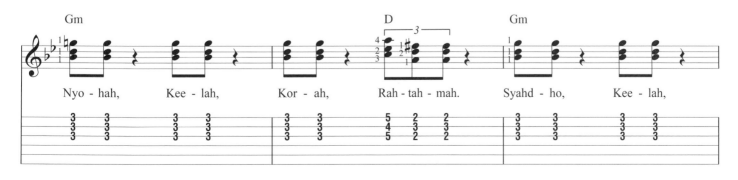

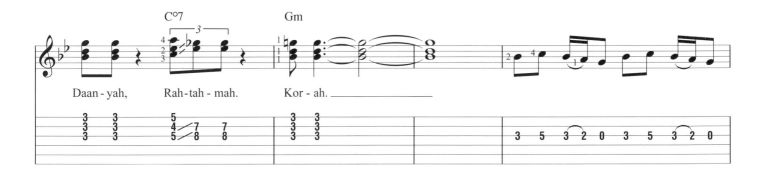

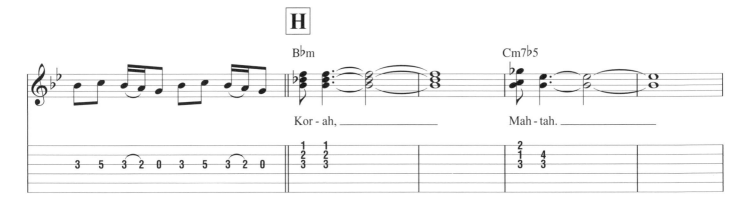

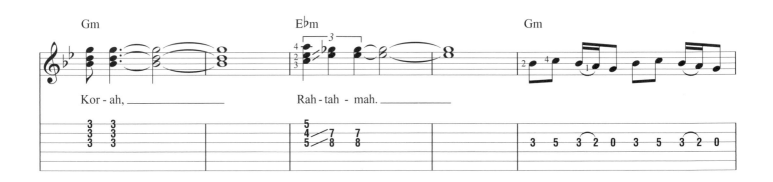

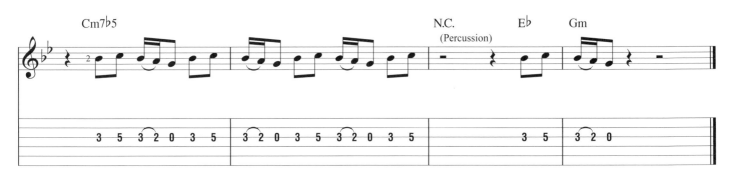

Han Solo and the Princess

Music by John Williams

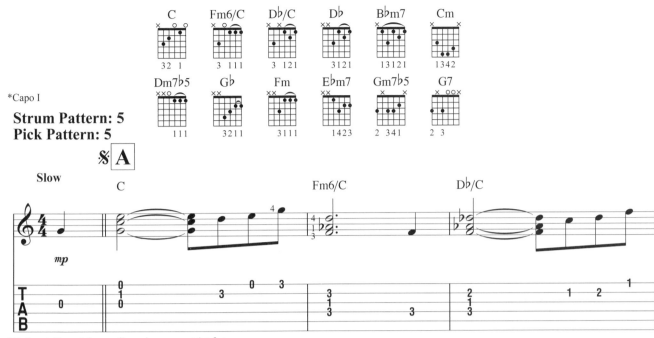

*Capo I

Strum Pattern: 5
Pick Pattern: 5

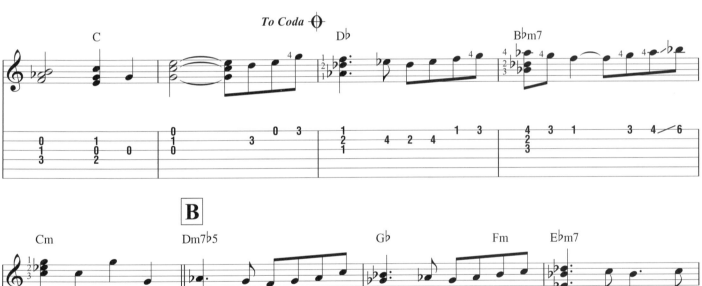

*Optional: To match recording, place capo at 1st fret.

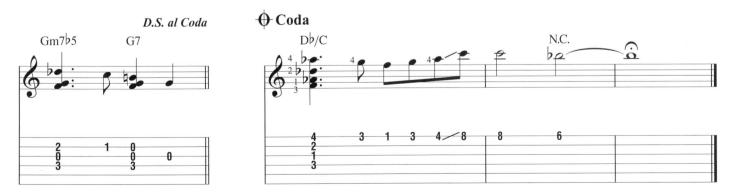

The Imperial March
(Darth Vader's Theme)

from THE EMPIRE STRIKES BACK - A Twentieth Century-Fox Release

Music by John Williams

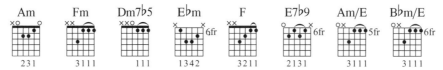

*Tune down 1 step:
(low to high) D-G-C-F-A-D

Strum Pattern: 3
Pick Pattern: 3

Intro
Moderately

*Optional: To match recording, tune down 1 step.
**Chord symbols reflect implied harmony.

% A

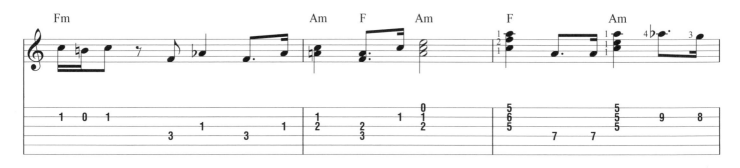

The Jedi Steps *and* Finale

from STAR WARS: THE FORCE AWAKENS
Music by John Williams

*Capo III

Strum Pattern: 5
Pick Pattern: 5

*Optional: To match recording, place capo at 3rd fret.

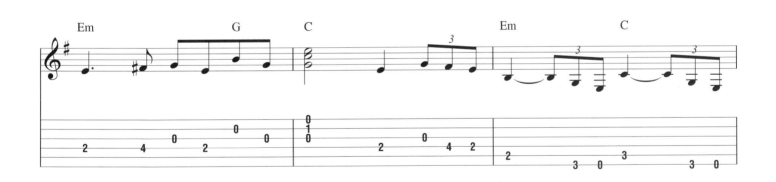

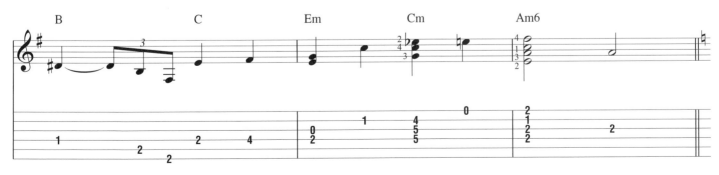

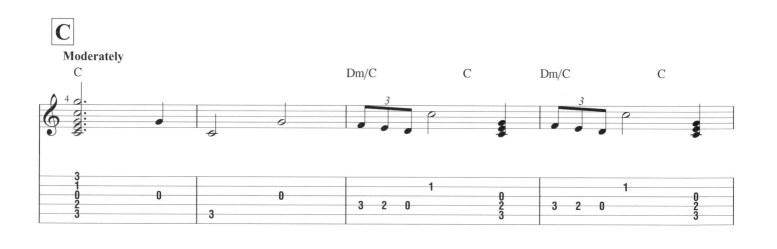

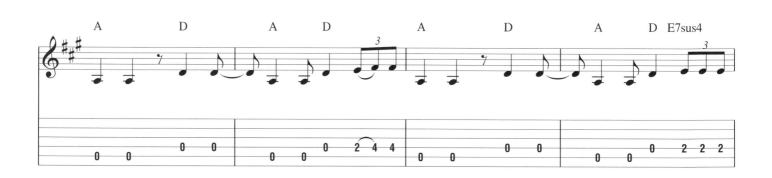

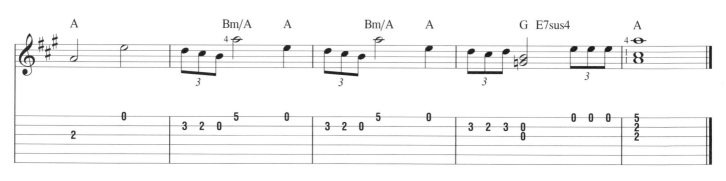

May the Force Be with You

Music by John Williams

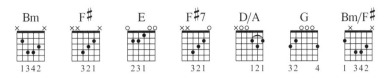

*Capo I

Strum Pattern: 3
Pick Pattern: 3

Moderately slow

*Optional: To match recording, place capo at 1st fret.

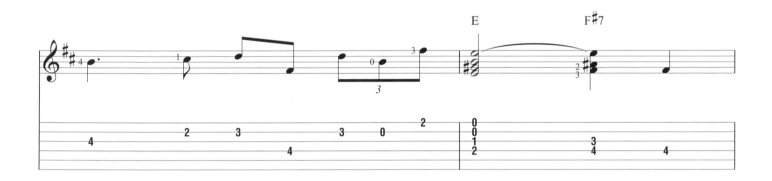

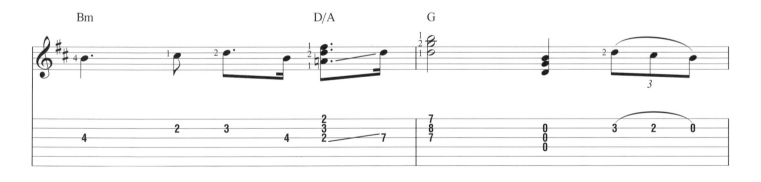

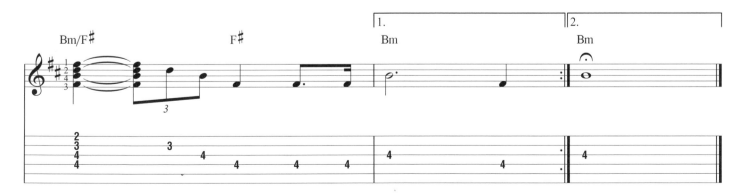

Luke and Leia

from STAR WARS: EPISODE VI - RETURN OF THE JEDI

Music by John Williams

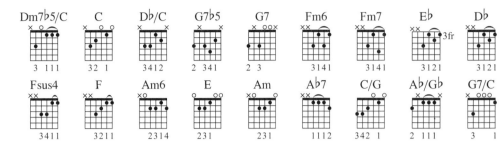

*Capo I

Strum Pattern: 3
Pick Pattern: 2

Moderately slow

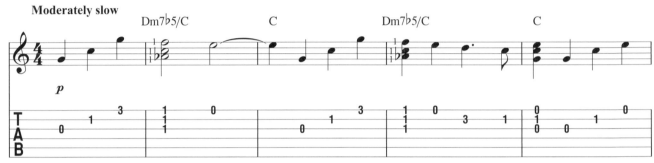

*Optional: To match recording, place capo at 1st fret.

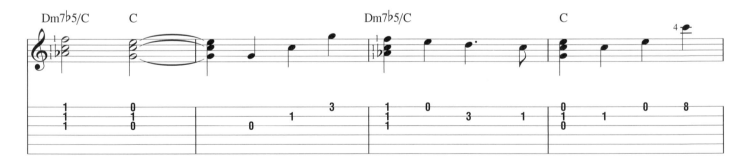

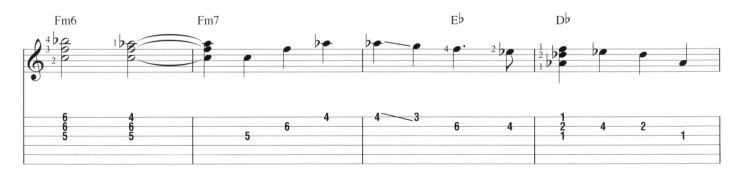

March of the Resistance

from STAR WARS: THE FORCE AWAKENS

Music by John Williams

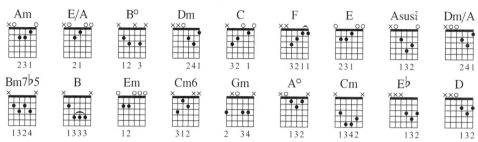

*Tune down 1 step:
(low to high) D-G-C-F-A-D

Strum Pattern: 5
Pick Pattern: 1

Moderately

*Optional: To match recording, tune down 1 step.

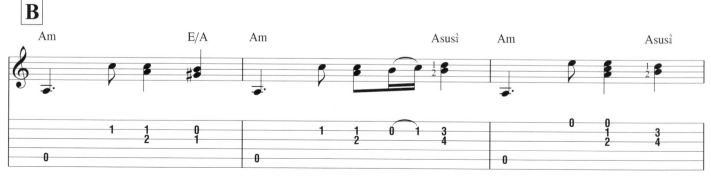

Princess Leia's Theme

from STAR WARS - A Twentieth Century-Fox Release

Music by John Williams

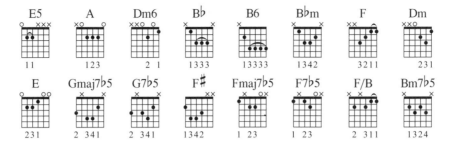

*Capo V

Strum Pattern: 1
Pick Pattern: 5

*Optional: To match recording, place capo at 5th fret.

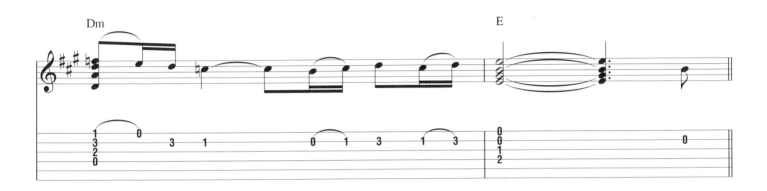

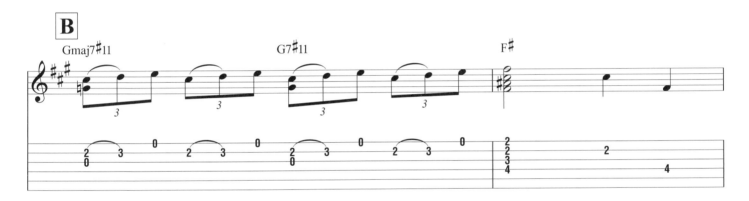

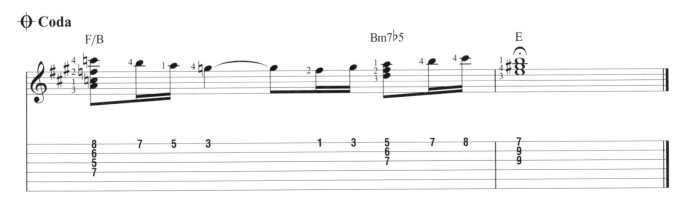

Rey's Theme

from STAR WARS: THE FORCE AWAKENS

Music by John Williams

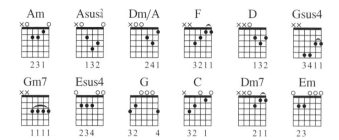

Strum Pattern: 5
Pick Pattern: 1

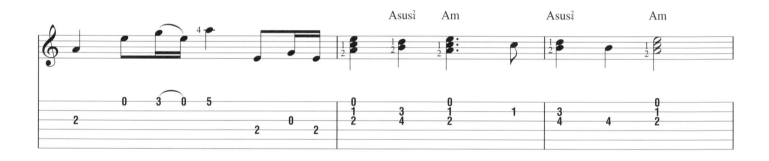

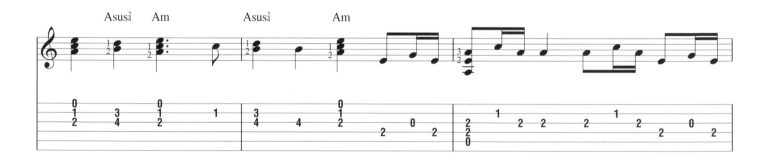

*T = Thumb on 6th string

Star Wars
(Main Theme)

from STAR WARS, THE EMPIRE STRIKES BACK and RETURN OF THE JEDI

Music by John Williams

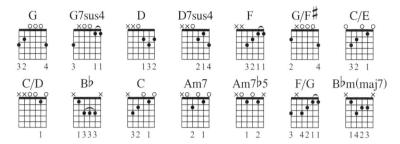

*Capo III

Strum Pattern: 4
Pick Pattern: 3

Intro
Moderately

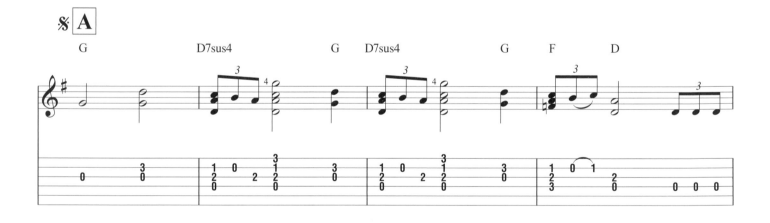

*Optional: To match recording, place capo at 3rd fret.

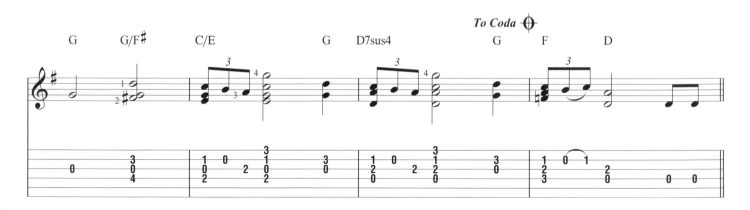

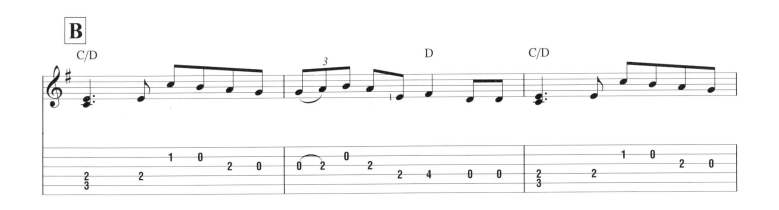

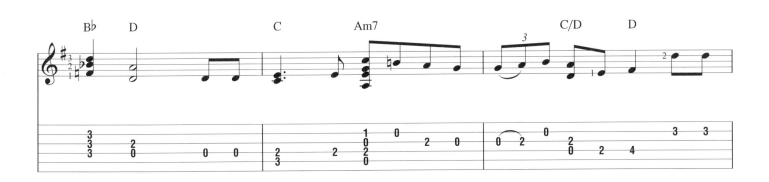

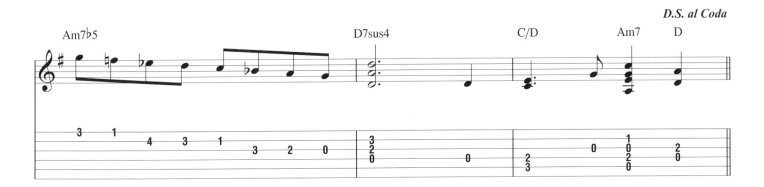

D.S. al Coda

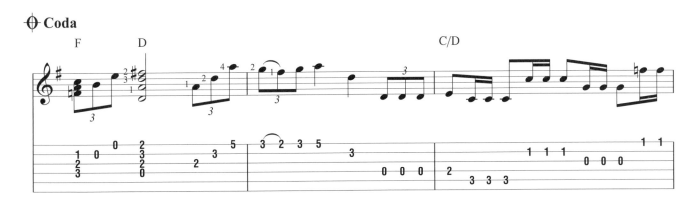

Coda

Yoda's Theme

from THE EMPIRE STRIKES BACK - A Twentieth Century-Fox Release

Music by John Williams

Strum Pattern: 4
Pick Pattern: 4

The Throne Room
(And End Title)

from STAR WARS: EPISODE IV - A NEW HOPE

Music by John Williams

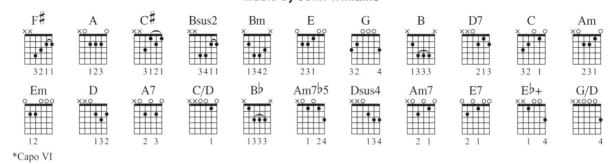

*Capo VI

Strum Pattern: 3
Pick Pattern: 3

Intro
Moderately

*Optional: To match recording, place capo at 6th fret.

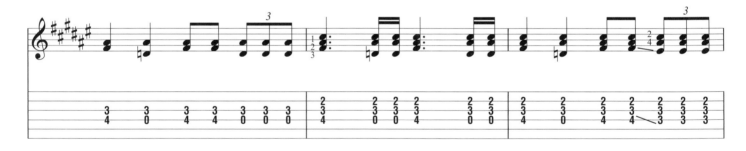

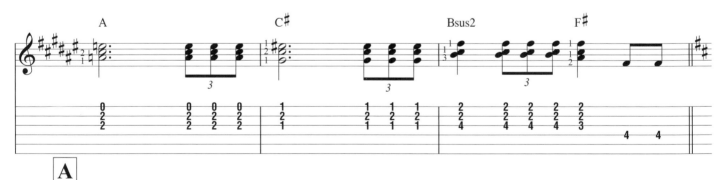

A

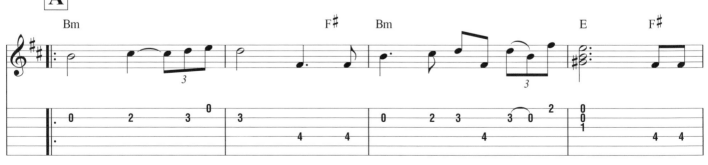

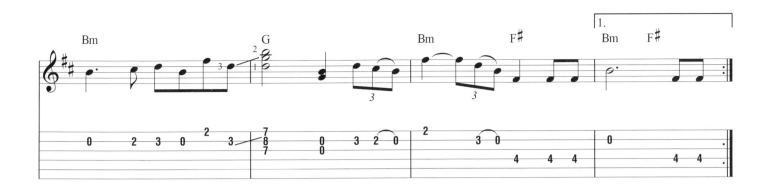

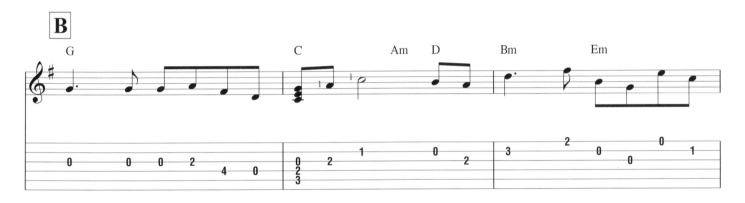

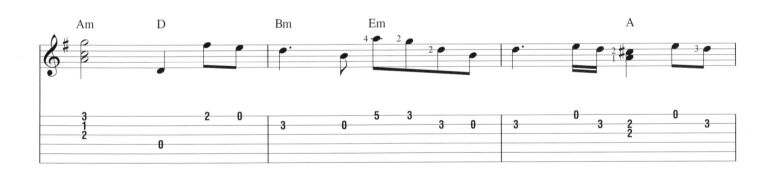

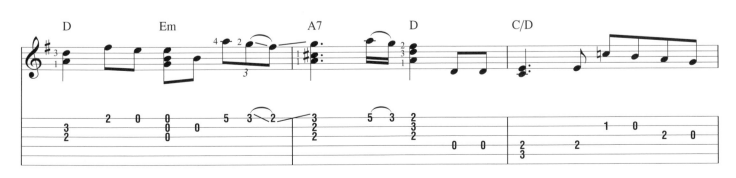

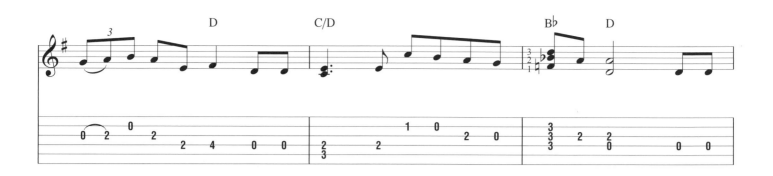

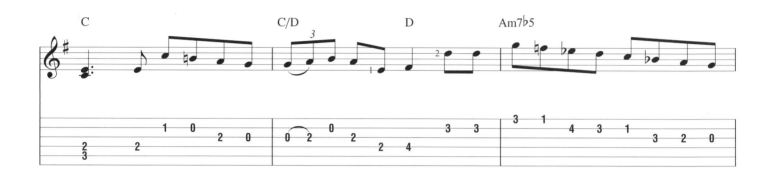

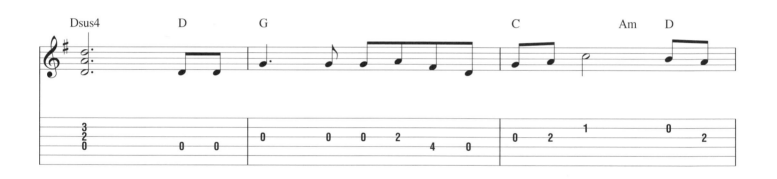

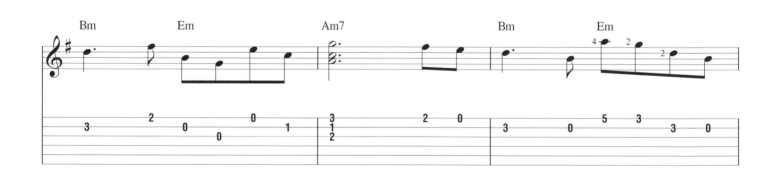

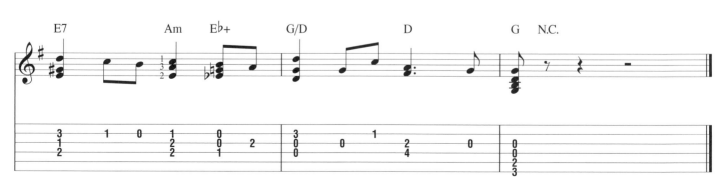